The Doctor Sebi Diet

The complete Guide to alkaline Diet With easy Doctor Sebi alkaline Recipes & Food List for Weight Loss, Liver cleansing

Table of contents

You don't have to eat less, you just have to **eat** right.

Dr. Sebi Rest in Power

INTRoDUcTIoN

Dr. Sebi was a Honduran man with a very humble beginning and was known and addressed as an herbalist, pathologist or a naturalist in different regions of the world; he left the biosphere in 2016. Indeed, it is true that he is no longer in our midst today, but his self-invented and established effective traditional therapy for diabetes, hypertension and organ cleansing is still helping millions of people with these conditions around the world. He created great strides in the world of natural health and wellness with the creation of his specialized diet.

Dr. Sebi said that there were six fundamental food groups: live, raw, dead, hybrid, genetically modified, and drugs, but his diet basically cut out all the food groups except live and raw food, thereby encouraging dieters to eat as closely to a raw vegan diet as possible.

These foods include foods like naturally grown fruits and vegetables, along with whole grains.

He has the believed that raw and live foods were "electric," which fought the acidic food waste in the body. So, with his approach to eating, Dr. Sebi established a list of foods that he deliberated to be the best for his diet.

Sticking to Dr Sebi's Diet and Food List to cure these diseases can be challenging if you eat out a lot. consequently, you need to get used to making lots of meals at home.

To help with this, this book was born so as to give you all of the information you need to eat right and the type of herbs to eat to live healthy.

This way you do not have to put too much thought into what you have to eat and the less thought you have to put into the diet, the easier it will become to stick to it.

This great herbalist during his lifetime cured a lot of diseased people and even after his death, he left an exceptional knowledge of holistic healing for diabetes, hypertension and organ cleansing. You too can be inspired from his life and the approach he perceived various terminal diseases. However, you might be worried about treating the above mentioned diseases, right?

of course, diabetes, hypertension are annoying health conditions that have no remedy in allopathy. This is the reason people are trying several different alternative medicines. Those who are new to this approach of eating are trying them to get total cure, while others already practicing this are just hoping to avoid the side effects of antiviral drugs.

Diabetes, hypertension and toxins have without doubt created many health problems in the lives of millions of people, but now is the time you should think about curing it rather than treating.

chapter [1]

HoW To NaTURaLLY ReVeRSe YoUR DIaBeTeS: THe eaT To LIVe pLaN oF DR. SeBI NaTURaL FooD GUIDe To eND DIaBeTeS

Diabetes mellitus is undoubtedly one of the fastest killing illnesses in america. This illnesses is caused when the kidney or the pituitary hormone cannot function effectively. The widespread of this disease has been attributed to a slight change otherwise referred to as a defect in the pancreas insulin production. Glucose and insulin are intertwined and being that the body cannot process glucose on its own, it needs insulin to help break down the ingested glucose. Diabetes has its origin rooted in ancient Greek, with its meaning being "pass through" or "flow through". a meaning which has been attributed to how often diabetes sufferers need to ease themselves.

on the other hand, the word mellitus means sweet. In short, diabetes mellitus (type 1, called insulin dependent diabetes) makes it impossible for the pancreas to produce the insulin needed to process the glucose in the body. Type 2 diabetes (insipidus diabetes, called non-insulin-dependent diabetes) also bring about the same flaw as the type 1 with the difference being that the pancreas produces enough insulin which the body finds it hard to process.

The forest not only hides man's enemies but it's full of man's medicine, healing power and food. ~african proverb

What can make us develop diabetes mellitus?

- Stress
- obesity
- pregnancy

Some types of drugs:

- adrenal corticosteroids
- Thiazide diuretics

- phenytoin

High sugar diet:

- Sugar

- White flour

- candy

- Foods containing processed sugar

Natural cures for diabetes:

The habit of over eating and eating late in the night should be stopped as it induces diabetes and makes the condition worse in people who already have it. Instead of depending on conventional everyday food, a diet of high fiber and high carbohydrates should be considered. This diet gradually eliminates the need for insulin. protein and vegetables should be a high priority while foods containing fats should not even find their way to your priority list. onions and other raw food has been proven to be advantageous to diabetes sufferers as these food has been proven to reduce blood sugar.

What to avoid that can worsen diabetes.

The following can lead to the development of diabetes or worsen diabetes:

- eggs
- Tobacco
- eating sugar
- cheese
- coffee
- cow's milk
- Meat
- Greasy foods
- White flour products
- Rancid nut or seed
- Too much vegetable oil
- Gluten foods such as wheat, barley, and oats

Here's Dr. Sebi's natural food guide for more food you can rely on.

Natural herbs to help with diabetes:

The best way to ease your diabetes situation is to exercise a lot. This act helps with blood circulation to keep you away from a visit to the doctor.

- Black walnut, echinacea, burdock root, and buchu help alleviate diabetes
- Huckleberry improves the production of insulin
- Dandelion root helps to reduce blood sugar
- cedar berries gives the pancreas needed strength

Dr. Sebi natural food guide is helpful for treating diabetes

The safest and easily accessible food for diabetic people are fresh raw vegetables, freshly made salad of raw vegetables such as plum tomatoes, cabbage and lettuce seasoned with seeded yellow lemon juice. Totally avoid meat, bread, cooked vegetables and processed junk foods. Raw food should be your breakfast, lunch and dinner.

Natural alkaline seeded raw fruits are highly advised. These fruits includes coconut water, pears, peaches, sour sop, and lemon juice which oxidizes the excess blood sugar in the body. You should as a matter of fact stay away from GMo seedless fruits as they are too sweet.

chapter [2]

BeST NaTURaL FooDS FoR LIVeR HeaLTH aND aLKaLINe DIeTS FRoM DR. SeBI'S NUTRITIoNaL FooD GUIDe LIST

The best foods for the healthy function of the liver is at the top of the best investments you can ever make for your body. The liver is a vital organ and it does more jobs than any other human organ. The liver handles a lot of chemically challenging activities with their own complexities. Basically, the liver is responsible for distributing numerous chemicals to intended places in order to provide energy. a diet that consists of clean foods is good for the health of the liver as this will keep it working optimally.

Here are some proven foods for liver and health nutrition.

Foods for good liver functionality:

The foods suggested for liver health are alkaline, natural, GMo-free and organic foods. They are rich in minerals and compliment the body's biological molecular structure.

Here are some potassium-rich foods for liver health:

- Banana

- prunes and

- Raisins

Water is inarguably the best food for liver health

- Divide your body weight by two and take that number in ounces of pure natural spring water.

Juices and raw fresh vegetables for liver health

- Dandelion greens
- amaranth greens

- Rosemary
- okra

- plum tomatoes
- cabbage and
- Fennel

Raw nuts is good for a healthy liver

- Brazil nuts
- Hazel nuts
- Walnuts and

- almond

Fruit juices are excellent nutrients for liver function:

- apple juice - fresh and natural
- Fresh prune juice
- Ginger juice

- Lemon juice

Why were the above foods chosen for liver health and functionality?

- apples make the liver efficient in its processes

- Dandelion helps to cleanse the liver
- Ginger contains eight compounds that defends the liver
- Lemon juice aids in carrying oxygen to the liver in a bid to get rid of all fatty buildup
- prune juice flushes every impurity from the liver
- Rosemary helps rejuvenates a weak liver

Now that you know how important the liver is, here are more reasons why you should eat only foods that are best for its optimal function. The liver is a gland that is responsible for getting rid of toxins in the body. This is the reason why priority should be given to your liver's health and functionality as doing otherwise will deprive the liver of its ability to store and conserve energy. Because I am a staunch believer of the liver's health and optimal function, I will take this book beyond its original scope of healthy foods for the liver.

Herbs for good liver health and function:

- Bayberry
- Dandelion
- Lobelia

- parsley and
- Yellow dock

chapter [3]

eXcepTIoNaL STRaTeGIeS oF DR. SeBI'S HIGH BLooD pReSSURe DIeT, HoW To LoWeR SYMpToMS oF HIGH BLooD pReSSURe, aND WHaT caUSeS HYpeRTeNSIoN

What is high blood pressure?

If the walls of the arteries were to be clogged or packed with plagues, the flow of blood will become restricted as it pumps from the heart to the aorta, when the arteries creates pressure in a situation like this, the blood pressure becomes higher than it should be and this results into hypertension (high blood pressure).

poor diet is the leading cause of high blood pressure in the United States as it has been reported that over 85 percent reported high blood pressure cases are rooted in poor diet. More than any other race in the United States, african americans reported more cases of having a high blood pressure. High blood pressure is a channel to other diseases such as kidney diseases, strokes, scarlet fever, large heart, typhoid fever, artery coronary diseases and tonsillitis. These diseases are rampant among african americans who have a hypertensive health history.

What is considered to be high blood pressure?

To be certain of your blood pressure, you will need a blood pressure gauge for accuracy. This gauge is often called a sphygmomanometer and it records two basic types of information: the first being systolic which is the higher reading while the second is diastolic which is the lower reading.

consequently, the diastolic high blood pressure is less worrisome than the systolic high blood pressure readings as the systolic shows the pressure of the blood built as it is being pumped through the passage ways in the arteries to the aorta. The blood pressure is definitely high when your systolic reading is high as a result of the artery walls being clogged thereby limiting blood flows. a normal systolic high blood pressure reading is usually between 120 – 150 millimeters. on the other hand, a high reading is 140/190; the indication of a systolic high blood pressure reading is over 180/115.

What causes high blood pressure?

High blood pressure is caused when the blood flowing to the arteries is high due to the consumption of foods that are capable of clogging the wall of the arteries. an act which results in a pressure through the arteries during the distribution of blood flow. Blood is pumped by the heart to the aorta then the arteries. peradventure the walls of the arteries become narrow and hardened due to excessive plague caused by poor eating habits, the flow of blood in the passageway of the arteries suppresses. Worthy of note is the fact that as an individual gets older, the arteries gets hardened bit by bit and a bad diet will triple the possibility of a high blood pressure.

Some of the numerous causes of high blood pressure:

asides clogged arteries, high blood pressure can also be cause by poor blood circulation. Synthetic drugs, processed foods and unhealthy behavior patterns also cause high blood pressure.

These behavioral pattern includes the following:

- Bad diet
- Tobacco intake

- Stress

- excess coffee intake
- Fried and processed foods

- over-eating
- aging

Symptoms of High Blood pressure:

according to Dr. Sebi, high blood pressure symptoms can be likened to "navy seal snipers" as there are no signs that a person's blood pressure is high. The few noticeable pointers of high blood pressure has always been difficulty in breathing, blurry vision, rapid pulses and incessant headache.

My mother when alive had high blood pressure, she once told me that her blood pressure symptoms are dizziness and that her pulse gets fast often. But, because high blood pressure symptoms are not always perceptible, it was given a nick name "the navy seal sniper killer."

Dr. Sebi High blood pressure diet:

- every high blood pressure drug in the market imitates water. This is why it is important for you as an individual to drink a lot of clean water. For this to be effective, you will need to divide your weight by 2 and drink that much water daily. Why that much water? You may ask. Well, water thins the blood and makes passing through the arteries easy.

- Taking five different types of fruits (vegetables included) a day will prevent the arteries from getting clogged as a result of excess plague deposits. Fruits and vegetables that contains a high percentage of antioxidant protects the artery walls from plague deposits. Such fruits include cabbage, tomatoes, oranges, seeded grapes and peaches.

- Foods that are rich in potassium helps to reduce recurrent high blood pressure as it expels excess sodium from the body.

- Fiber containing fruits are also of high benefit to high blood pressure sufferers as itwill lower the blood pressure while removing wastes from the artery walls at the same time.

High blood pressure after eating:

Food related high blood pressure knowledge is important as having no knowledge of what foods to eat and the ones to avoid is detrimental to the blood pressure level. No one wants to get a high blood pressure from eating like everybody else. Here are some food to avoid:

- avoid overeating even the healthiest of food.
- avoid salty foods as much as possible as they transform into plaque in the artery walls. In essence, avoid sodas, baking soda, soy sauce and meat tenderizers.

- Never eat canned foods.
- eliminate dairy products such as sodium, cheese and alcohol from your diet.
- Do not eat in the evening
- avoid every other type of rice except wild and brown

Dr. Sebi High blood pressure medication (natural herbs):

These herbs are recommended by Dr. Sebi as they help to open the blood vessels, open the arteries walls and eliminate plaques from the wall of arteries. These herbs contain natural alkaline and are high in minerals. These are not hearsays, they have been medically proved to be effective as blood pressure medication. These herbals are usually high in iron, some of these herbs include;

- Fennel
- oregano
- Basil

- Yellow dock

- cayenne

chapter 4

DR. SeBI eLecTRIc FooD LIST

DR. SeBI FRUIT LIST

- apples

- Bananas
- Berries
- cantaloupe
- cherries
- currants
- Dates
- Figs
- Grapes
- Limes
- Mango
- Melons
- orange
- papayas
- peaches
- pears
- plums
- prickly pear
- prunes
- Rasins
- Soft Jelly coconuts
- Soursoups

- Tamarind

DR. SeBI VeGeTaBLe LIST

- amaranth

- arame
- avocado
- Bell pepper
- chayote
- cherry and plum Tomato
- cucumber
- Dandelion Greens
- Dulse
- Garbanzo Beans
- Hijiki
- Izote flower and leaf
- Kale
- Lettuce except iceberg
- Mushrooms except Shitake
- Nopales
- Nori
- okra
- olives
- onions
- purslane Verdolaga
- Squash
- Tomatillo
- Turnip Greens
- Wakame
- Watercress
- Wild arugula

- Zucchini

DR. SeBI HeRB LIST

- Basil

- cayenne
- Dill
- onion powder
- oregano

- pure sea salt

aLKaLINe SUGaRS aND SWeeTeNeRS

- Date Sugar from dried dates

- 100% pure agave Syrup from cactus

DR SeBI HeRBaL TeaS

- Burdock

- chamomile
- elderberry
- Fennel
- Ginger
- Red Raspberry

- Tila

DR. SeBI aLKaLINe GRaINS

- amaranth

- Fonio
- Kamut
- Quinoa
- Rye
- Spelt
- Tef

- Wild Rice

DR SeBI FooD LIST oF SpIceS aND SeaSoNINGS

- achiote

- Basil
- Bay Leaf
- cayenne
- cloves
- Dill
- Habanero
- onion powder
- oregano
- powdered Granulated Seaweed
- pure Sea Salt
- Sage
- Savory
- Sweet Basil
- Tarragon
- Thyme

DR.SeBI aLKaLINe RecIpeS

DR. SeBI BaRBecUe SaUce RecIpe

This recipe makes about 8-10 oz. of barbecue sauce.

Ingredients

- 2 tsp. onion powder
- 2 tbsp. agave
- 1/4 cup White onions, chopped
- 1/4 tsp. cayenne powder
- 2 tsp. Smoked Sea Salt/Sea Salt
- 6 plum Tomatoes
- 1/8 tsp. cloves
- Blender
- Hand Mixer
- 1/4 cup Date Sugar
- 1/2 tsp. Ground Ginger

The longer you allow this recipe to set, the better it tastes.

preparation

1. Set aside date sugar then toss all the other ingredients into a blender and blend until smooth.
2. once the ingredients have been properly blended, combine them with date sugar then toss into a saucepan at medium-high heat. Stir occasionally until boiling.
3. once the mix has reached a boiling state, cover the saucepan, then reduce the lid and allow to simmer for 15 minutes.
4. To make the sauce smoother, consider using a stick blender.
5. To steam off the remnant water, simmer on low heat for another 10 minutes.
6. Before you serve, make sure the sauce has cooled off and it has thickened to your desired state.
7. Now that your alkaline Barbecue sauce is ready, enjoy however you wish.

DR. SeBI SpRING RoLLS RecIpe

Ingredients

- Spelt Flour
- Kale
- Red peppers
- alkaline orange Ginger Sauce (optional)
- Green peppers
- Grapeseed oil
- Sea Salt
- Lime Juice
- Spring Water
- Red onions
- onion powder
- avocados

- aquafaba (chickpea Water) (optional)

Materials Needed

- Masher
- parchment paper

- 6-inch Food Scraper
- Wooden Dowel or Rolling pin

- Food processor

Kale Filling

This Kale filling should be enough to prepare 6 spring rolls.

Measurements:

- 2 tsp. Grapeseed oil
- 1 tsp. Sea Salt
- 3 cups Kale
- 1/2 cup red onions, sliced
- 1/2 of red pepper, thinly sliced

- 1 tsp. onion powder

preparation

Set your cooker to medium heat then place a skillet on it. add all the ingredients in the skillet then saute for 7 minutes until the vegetables starts to get tender.

avocado Filling

Depending on the size of the avocado, this filling should be enough to make about 5 to 6 spring rolls.

Measurements:

- 2 tbsp. Green peppers, diced
- 1/2 tsp. Sea Salt

- 1 avocado
- 1 tsp. Lime Juice
- 1 tsp. onion powder

- 2 tbsp. Red onions, diced

To make things easier and faster, divide the avocado in halves, do away with the seed then scoop out the insides into a suitable bowl.

Toss in the other ingredients into the bowl, mix together thoroughly then mash.

Spring Rolls

only a maximum of 12 spring rolls can be gotten from this recipe.

Measurements:

- 1/3 cup Grapeseed oil
- 1 tsp. onion powder
- 1/2 cup Spring Water
- 2 cups Spelt Flour

- 1 tsp. Sea Salt

Direction for preparations:

1. clean your food processor, toss in seasonings and flour into it then blend for 10 seconds.
2. Drizzle grapeseed oil while mixing.
3. add little drops of water while mixing until the dough now forms a ball.
4. Knead the dough then with the help of a food scraper, separate the dough into 5 parts.
5. Form out a thin circle with the dough then cut out a 6-inch square with your food scraper. Repeat this process to form the remaining dough.
6. To avoid the cut squares from sticking together, place parchment paper in between the squares.
7. To allow the doughs stick together, brush the corners and edges with spring water(or aquafaba) before rolling.
8. each roll should have about 2-3 tablespoons of filling.
9. place the dough like a diamond the tuck in the filling in one of its corners, fold both the left and the right side such that they meet in the center then roll forward. The roll should be tightly done in order to allow for ease of picking it up.

10. Set your cooker to medium heat then coat the skillet lightly with grapeseed oil.
11. place the rolls into the skillet then cook each side for a minute with the help of tongs.
12. after the two main sides are done, place the rolls upright on each side for a minute. This is to allow all 4 sides to get properly cooked.
13. To optimally enjoy your alkaline Spring Rolls, you should consider serving with our orange Ginger Sauce.

DR. SeBI KaLe cHIpS RecIpe

This recipe makes about 2 - 4 servings.

Ingredients

- onion powder (optional)
- Grapeseed oil
- 1 lb. Kale
- cayenne (optional)

- Sea Salt

To get the most out of this recipe, it is advised that you rinse your kale a day before making the kale chips. This is in order to allow the kale dry up properly before use.

Direction for preparations

1. Your oven should be preheated to 350°F.

2. properly rinse the kale then dry it off with paper towels or hair dryer depending on what you have available in your household.

3. Grab a pair of scissors then cut off the kale leaves very close to the stem. ensure you do not cut the leaves in small sizes as they have been reputed to shrink in size when cooked.

4. Toss seasoning into a bowl then add the kale. Drizzle enough oil to coat the content of the bowl.

5. Toss the kale gently with tongs.

6. Grab a baking sheet then place the kale on it. place the kale and the baking sheet in an oven then allow to bake for 8 minutes.

7. Repeat this process until you have no kale left to bake. Thereafter, you can enjoy your delicious kale chips.

DR. SeBI HeMp SeeD MaYo RecIpe

The mayo recipe should amount to 1 ½ cups of mayo.

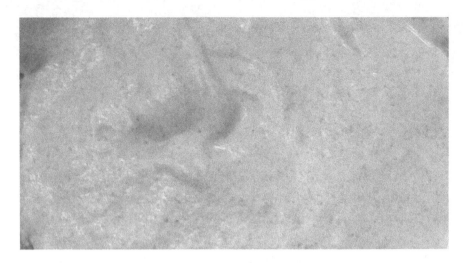

Ingredients

- cup Blender or Stick Blender
- 3/4 cup Spring Water
- 1/2 tsp. Sea Salt
- 1 cup Hemp Seeds
- 1 tsp. Lime Juice
- 1 tbsp. onion powder

- 2 tbsp. Grape Seed oil

Direction for preparations

1. Toss in all the ingredients into the cup blender then allow to blend for a minute until the texture is smooth.
2. If the texture of the blended ingredient is too thick, add some water to achieve desired texture. on the

other hand, if the texture is too light, you can add some hemp seed to thicken it.

3. This hemp seed mayo mixture should be stored in an air-tight container and kept in a refrigerator.

4. Whenever you have the need for the mayo, take it out of the refrigerator and serve.

DR. SeBI VeGaN pIZZa RecIpe

The nature of this recipe makes it that it will turn out to be a thin-crust.

Ingredients

- avocado
- Green / Red Bell pepper
- Brazil Nut cheese
- oregano
- Food processor or Blender
- Red / White onions
- Grapeseed oil

- Spelt Flour

- Mushrooms
- onion powder
- Sea Salt
- agave Nectar
- Roma Tomatoes

alkaline pizza crust

Measurements:

- 1 tsp. oregano
- 1 cup Spring Water

- 1 1/2 cups Spelt Flour
- 1 tsp. onion powder
- 2 tsp. agave
- 1 tsp. Sea Salt
- 2 tsp. Grapeseed oil
- 2 tsp. Sesame seeds

Direction for preparation

1. preheat your oven to 400°F.
2. Grab a medium sized bowl, add ½ cup of water then toss in all the other ingredients. add drops of water until you can mi the dough into a ball. If the mix is watery, add some more flour to achieve desired texture.
3. Sprinkle some grapeseed oil on your baking sheet. Rub some flour on your palm then roll out the dough into the baking sheet.
4. Grab a fork then poke holes on top of the crust. Sprinkle some grapeseed oil on it afterwards. Bake the crust for a minimum of 10 minutes and maximum of 15 minutes.

5. While the crust is baking, prepare either a tomato or an avocado sauce as outlined in the recipe guide below.
6. once the crust has been properly baked, add the onions, peppers, mushrooms, Brazil nut cheese and pizza sauce. Then bake again for 20 minutes.
7. Take your pizza out of the oven then serve as desired.

The presence of nut cheese in this recipe is to aid thorough cooking of the toppings while baking. In the scenario that you do not have nut cheese around, you can opt for sautéing the toppings lightly before baking. If you are interested in making brazil nut cheese, the recipe can be found here.

DR. SeBI DaTe SUGaR RecIpe

This electric date sugar recipe can only yield a maximum of 1 ½ cups.

Ingredients

- Baking Sheet
- Blender/Food processor

- 8 oz. Dates

To make use of the date, you can either remove the seeds or leave them be. Your baking time will be determined by how large your dates are. The larger your dates, the longer you bake.

Direction for preparations

1. pre-heat your oven to 400°F
2. If you don't want the seeds, cut the dates in half then get rid of them. (This step is sticky)
3. carefully place the dates on a cooking sheet.
4. The dates are to be baked for a maximum of 15 minutes. Thereafter, they will appear slightly burnt. Try as much as possible to not overcook them.
5. once you are done baking the dates, allow them to completely cool off.
6. after being cooled off, the dates should be as hard as candy. If yours is not hard after it has been cooled off, bake the dates again for another 5 minutes.
7. place the dates in a blender then blend for 10 seconds.

8. Your alkaline date sugar is now ready to be served.

DR. SeBI STUFFeD GReeN peppeR RecIpe

This recipe yields 4 - 6 servings, depending upon the size of the peppers.

Ingredients

- 1/2 White onion, chopped
- 1 Tsp. Sea Salt
- 1 Tsp. onion powder
- 4-6 Bell peppers
- 2 plum Tomatoes, Diced
- 1 1/2 cup Brazil Nut cheese
- 1 cup Tomato Sauce
- 2 cups of cooked Wild Rice
- 1/2 Tsp. cayenne powder
- 1/2 Red / purple onion, chopped
- 1 Tsp. oregano
- 1-2 Tbsp. Grapeseed oil

- 1/2 lb. Mushrooms, Sliced

Direction for preparations

1.peppers

a.cut away the tops of the ball peppers then do away with the seeds and the flesh.

b.Heat water to boiling point then place the peppers in it for 5 minutes. This is to soften up the pepper.

c.once it has softened up, remove from the water then place into a baking pan. Sprinkle 1 tablespoon of sea salt on it.

2.Vegetables

.Set your cooker to medium-high heat then place a large skillet on it. Sprinkle 1 tablespoon of grapeseed oil in the skillet.

a.Toss in seasonings, mushrooms and onions into the skillet. Mix these ingredients and saute for 5 minutes.

3.add 1 cup of Brazil nut cheese, ½ of your tomato sauce, wild rice and plum tomatoes then allow to simmer for 5 minutes.

4.Stuff the peppers with the sautéed mix then use Brazil nut cheese and the remaining tomato sauce as toppings.

5.Set your oven to 350°F then bake for a maximum of 30 minutes.

6.after the baking, your alkaline stuffed green peppers is now ready to be served.

DR. SeBI RaW TaHINI BUTTeR RecIpe

Materials and Ingredients

- blender
- 1 - 2 tablespoons grapeseed oil

- 1 cup raw sesame seeds

Direction for preparations

1. Grab your blender then toss in the raw sesame seeds into the blender cup
2. Blend the seeds until the mix becomes chunky
3. add some oil
4. Blend until you achieve a buttery texture

5. Store in an air-tight container then keep in a refrigerator.

DR. SeBI RoaSTeD ToMaTo SaUce RecIpe

This electric roasted tomato sauce recipe will only yield a maximum of 6 cups.

Ingredients

- 2 teaspoons onion powder
- 1 medium shallot

- 18 roma tomatoes
- 1 tablespoon agave
- 1/8 cup grapeseed oil
- 3 teaspoons basil
- 2 teaspoons oregano
- 1/2 red onion
- 1/2 red bell pepper
- 3 teaspoons sea salt
- 1/8 teaspoon cayenne powder
- 1/2 sweet onion

equipment

- parchment paper

- cookie sheet
- pot – at least 4 Quart

- Blender

Direction for preparation

1. pre-heat your oven to 400° F.
2. Grab all your vegetables and cut them in half. place them in a mixing bowl afterwards. cut all vegetables in half and place in mixing bowl.
3. add a tablespoon of oil and basil then add grapeseed oil according to your need.
4. add vegetables to the mixtures until they are fully coated.
5. place the cut side of all the vegetables on a cookie sheet lined with parchment paper.
6. place the cooking sheet and parchment paper in the oven and allow to bake for 30 minutes. Turn the cookie sheet halfway through the cooking.
7. Toss the roasted vegetables in a blender then blend om high speed until a smooth texture is achieved.
8. pour out the blended mix and all other ingredients into a pot then cook on low heat for 20 minutes.

DR. SeBI HeRBaL GLUTeN-FRee BReaD RecIpe

This gluten-free herb bread can only yield 1 loaf.

Ingredients

- 1 tsp. oregano
- 1 tsp Thyme
- 1/2 cup alkaline electric Date Syrup
- 1 tsp. Basil
- equipment
- 1 tbsp. onion powder
- 9" x 5" Loaf pan
- 1 1/2 cups Sparkling Spring Water
- 4 cups chickpea Flour
- Mixing Bowl
- 1 tbsp. Sea Salt

- 3 tbsp. Grapeseed oil

Direction for preparation

1. place all the dry ingredients in a mixing bowl then blend.
2. add 1 cup of sparkling spring water, grapeseed oil and date syrup then stir gently.
3. If your batter is not pourable and looks nothing like a cake batter then it is too thick. add more

sparkling spring water to reduce its thickness and to make the batter pourable.

4. Grab a loaf pan then pour in the batter. Grapeseed oil and herbs of your choosing can be used as topping.

5. Set your oven to 350 º then place in the loaf pan. Bake for a maximum of 60 minutes.

6. Your alkaline electric gluten-free herb bread is now ready to be served as desired.

DR. SeBI poT pIe RecIpe

This alkaline electric pot pie recipe will yield a maximum of 6 servings.

Ingredients

- •Hemp Milk
- Sea Salt

- Quinoa Flour
- Garbanzo Bean Four
- cayenne powder
- Kale
- cooked Garbanzo Beans
- Grapeseed oil
- Red & Green Bell pepper
- Red & White onion
- Savory
- oregano
- Mushrooms
- Spring Water
- Butternut Squash
- onion powder
- Basil
- Spelt Flour

Materials

- 8x8 Baking Dish
- Whisk
- Rolling Mat (optional)
- Food processor
- Wooden Dowel or Rolling pin

pot pie Filling

Measurements:

- •2 cups Mushrooms, chopped
- 1/2 cup Red & Green Bell pepper, diced
- 1-2 tbsp. Grapeseed oil
- 1/2 cup Red & White onion, diced
- 1/2 cup Spring Water*

- 1 cup cooked Garbanzo Beans
- 1 tsp. oregano
- 1 cup Butternut Squash, chopped
- 1/4 cup Garbanzo Bean Four*
- 1 tsp. onion powder
- 1 tsp. Basil
- 1/4 tsp. cayenne powder
- 1 tsp. Savory
- 1 cup Hemp Milk
- 1 tsp. Sea Salt
- 1 cup Kale, chopped

There is a high probability that you won't make use of all the available flour and water.

Direction for preparation:

1. Set your cooker to medium heat then place a large skillet on it. Sprinkle grapeseed oil in the skillet then sautee for 3 minutes.
2. add desired quantity of milk the slowly add garbanzo bean flour and whisk until the sauce thickens.
3. If your sauce turns out to be too thick, add some spring water to achieve desired texture.
4. Reduce the heat of your cooker to low then toss in vegetables and seasonings. cover with a lid and allow it to simmer for 15 minutes.

pie crusts

Measurements:

- 1/3 cup Grapeseed oil
- 1 tsp. Sea Salt

- 1 cup Spelt Flour
- 1 cup Quinoa Flour*
- 1 tsp onion powder
- 1/2 cup Spring Water

*To make the crusts extra flakey, Quinoa flour should be used. alternatively, you can use 2 cups spelt flour to achieve the same result.

Direction for preparation

1. Grab your food processor then add flour and seasonings. allow the mix to blend for 10 seconds. alternatively, you can mix the ingredients together in a bowl.
2. Drizzle grapeseed oil on the ingredients while mixing.
3. add little quantity of water to the dough until it forms a ball.
4. Sprinkle flour on your work area, divide the dough in half and roll it out thinly.
5. coat the baking dish lightly with oil and lay in the first crust.
6. The overlapping edges on the baking dish should be trimmed off. Thereafter, add pie filling.
7. The second crust should be laid on the baking dish. pinch the edges down and trim off the excess.
8. Set your oven to 350° the bake for 30 minutes.
9. Your alkaline pot pie is now ready to be served as desired.

DR. SeBI MaNGo SaLSa RecIpe

This mango salsa recipe will only yield a maximum of 3 cups.

Ingredients

- 1 tsp. Sea Salt
- 6 Roma Tomatoes
- 1 tsp. onion powder
- Juice from 1/2 of a Lime
- Food processor or Blender
- 1/2 cup cilantro
- 1/2 tsp. cayenne powder
- 1 Tomatillo
- 1/2 cup chopped Mango
- 1/4 cup Green peppers

- 1/2 cup Red onions

Direction for preparation

1. Grab your food processor then place all your ingredients in it except mango.

2. allow t to pulse for 10 seconds.
3. Scrap off the sides of the mango then add it to the other ingredients.
4. pulse again until the mango is thoroughly mixed with the salsa.

5. Your alkaline mango salsa is now ready to be served.

DR. SeBI appLe pIe RecIpe

This electric pie recipe can only yield 1 pie.

Ingredients

- 1/2 cup agave
- 1/4 tsp. Ground cloves
- 1/2 tsp. Sea Salt / 1 tsp. Sea Salt
- 1/3 cup Grapeseed oil
- 1/2 cup Date Sugar
- 2 cups Spelt Flour

- 3-4 lbs. baking apples
- 1/2 cup Spring Water
- 1 tsp. allspice
- Key limes (optional)

Materials

- pizza cutter
- apple Slicer/corer
- Food processor (optional)

- Vegetable peeler

This recipe was made with smith apples and gala apples. If you happen to not have a food processor, you can opt to mix the dough by hand.

Direction for preparation

1. pre-heat your oven to 425°F. Then, thinly slice your apples.
2. Grab a large skillet then add ½ sea salt, allspice, cloves, agave, date sugar and apples.
3. Set your cooker to medium-low. place your skillet on the cooker then add all the ingredients. allow o simmer for 20 minutes.
4. add 1 tablespoon of sea salt, and spelt flour to the food processor then allow to blend for 10 seconds.
5. While mixing, drizzle grapeseed oil and spring water until the dough forms a ball.
6. cut the dough into halves then roll out thinly. place the dough in a pie pan and remove excess dough.
7. Take a pinch of the apple mixture then taste. If needed, add more agave then transfer to the pie pan.

8. Grab the other half of the dough then roll it out. Take out a knife or pizza cutter to cut the dough into 1 inch strips.
9. place the strips horizontally across the pie, then place again vertically.
10. place in the oven then bake for a maximum of 35 minutes or until it turns golden brown.
11. Your alkaline apple pie is now ready to be served.

DR. SeBI eGG Foo YUNG RecIpe

This recipe can only make a maximum of 12 egg yung patties.

Ingredients

- 1/2 cup Red & White onion, chopped
- 1 cup Spring Water
- 1/2 cup Red & Green peppers, chopped
- 1 tsp. Sea Salt
- 1 tsp. Basil
- 2 cups Mushrooms, sliced
- 3/4 cup Garbanzo Bean Flour
- 1 tsp. oregano
- 1 cup Butternut Squash, chopped
- Grape Seed oil
- 1 tsp. onion powder
- 3 cups prepared Spaghetti Squash
- 1/2 tsp. cayenne powder
- 1/8 tsp. Ginger powder

- 1/2 cup Green onions, chopped

Direction for preparation

1. Grab a large bowl then whisk seasonings, water and garbanzo flour together in it.
2. Toss in spaghetti squash and chopped vegetables. Mix with hand until thoroughly blended
3. Set your cooker to high heat, place a large skillet on it. pour out grapeseed oil into the skillet then add ½ of the mixture.
4. pat the mixture down into patties then cook each side for a maximum of 4 minutes. add oil as needed.

5. Your electric egg Foo Yung Recipe is now ready to be served with fried rice. alkaline gravy or orange ginger sauce can be used as topping.

DR. SeBI SaLSa VeRDe RecIpe

This recipe will only amount to a maximum of 2 cups of salsa verde.

Ingredients

- •1 tsp. onion powder
- 1/4 cup Fresh cilantro
- Blender
- 1/2 cup onions
- 1 pound of Tomatillos
- 1 tsp. oregano
- Strainer
- 1 tsp. Sea Salt

Direction for preparation

1. Rinse the tomatilloes, remove the skin, rinse again then cut in half.
2. Set aside the cilantro then add the other ingredients into the saucepan. add enough water to cover the tomatilloes.
3. Set your cooker to medium-high heat then stir occasionally for 20 minutes.
4. Thoroughly strain the ingredients then add cilantro and the mixture to the blender. allow to blend for 30 seconds.
5. Your electric Salsa Verde is now ready to be served alongside alkaline spelt tortilla chips. This recipe can also be enjoyed with any dish of your choice.

DR. SeBI MaSHeD BUTTeRNUT SQUaSH RecIpe

This mashed squash recipe can only make a maximum of 6 servings.

Ingredients

- 1/4 cup organic Blue agave
- 1/8 tsp. Himalayan Sea Salt
- 1 tsp. allspice
- 1/4 cup Hemp Milk
- 2 Butternut Squashes

- 1/4 cup Date Sugar

Direction for preparation

1. cut off the ends of the butternut squash then grab a vegetable peeler to remove the skin.
2. cut the neck of the squash in half. Do same for the body of the squash.
3. Use a spoon to totally remove the seeds from the body
4. Slice the butternut squash into 1 inch chunks then place them in a pot.

5. add spring water until the squash is well covered. allow it to boil for 20 minutes or until the squash is tender.
6. Drain the water then mash the squash.
7. add sea salt. Date sugar, allspice, agave and hemp milk. Mix thoroughly.

8. Your Mashed Butternut Squash is now ready to be served as you wish.

DR. SeBI cHaYoTe MUSHRooM RecIpe

This electric chayote Mushroom Soup can only make a maximum of 8 servings

Ingredients

- Blender or Whisk
- 1 cup Hemp Milk
- 1 tbsp. onion powder

- 2 tsp. Sea Salt
- 1-2 tbsp. Grapeseed oil
- 3 cups Mushrooms, sliced
- 2 tsp. Basil
- 2 cups chayote Squash, cubed
- 1 tsp. crushed Red pepper

- 6 cups Spring Water
- 1 cup aquafaba or Vegetable Broth*
- 1 cup onions, diced
- 1 1/2 cups Garbanzo Bean Flour

- *If you have neither, you can use water*

Direction for preparation

1. Rinse the chayote squash, remove the skin then cut into cubes.
2. Set your cooker to medium-high then add grapeseed oil to sautee the mushrooms and onions.
3. add seasonings, aquafaba, milk, chayote and 4 springs of water then stir. cover with lid.
4. Grab your blender, add garbanzo bean flour and the remaining 2 cups of water. Blend for 20 seconds until there are no lumps. alternatively, you can whisk the ingredients together in a bowl.
5. Set your cooker to low heat, place a pot on it, pour out your mixture into the pot then allow to cook for 30 minutes.
6. Your alkaline electric chayote Mushroom Soup is now ready to be served.

DR. SeBI HoMeMaDe paSTa RecIpe

This recipe can only provide a maximum of 4 servings

Ingredients

- 1/2 tsp. Sea Salt

- 2 cups Spelt Flour/Kamut Flour*
- Grape Seed oil
- pastry cutter/pizza cutter
- 3/4 cup Spring Water, warm

- Roller/Dowel

Set aside 1 cup of flour for handling your dough and coating rolling pin.

Direction for preparation

1. Grab a large bowl, mix together salt, flour and ¼ cup of warm water until a ball is formed.
2. Sprinkle flour on your work area, then knead the dough for 8 minutes.
3. Use flour as coating for the plastic wrap and dough ball, allow the dough to set for 20 minutes.
4. Unwrap the dough then divide into 3 or 4 parts. Set aside the dough you are not using then rewrap them.
5. Roll out the dough in one direction a few times, flip the dough and repeat. after every flip, coat the area and dough with more flour.
6. Grab your pastry cutter then cut dough into desired shapes. (watch the video below to see how to cut the dough into desired shapes)
7. place a pot of water on your cooker then bring to boil. add sea salt and oil to the water. pour in your pasta, allow to cook for a minute then strain.

8. Your pasta is now ready to be served.

DR. SeBI RaVIoLI RecIpe

This recipe can make a maximum of 40 ravioli.

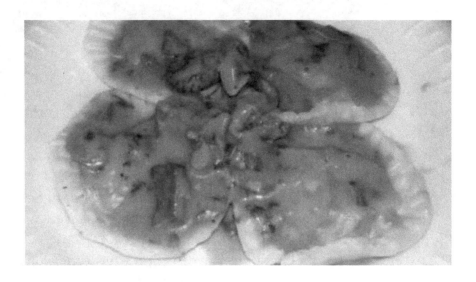

Ingredients

Ravioli Filling

- 2 tsp. Fennel Seeds
- 1 tsp. Ginger
- 2 tsp. oregano
- 2 tsp. Dill
- 2 tsp. Basil
- 1/3 cup onions, diced
- 2 cups Mushrooms, sliced
- 1 cup Kale, chopped
- 1/3 cup Green Bell pepper, diced
- 1 Roma Tomato
- 1 tsp. Sea Salt
- 1 cup Garbanzo bean flour
- 1/2 tsp. crushed Red pepper
- 1/2 tsp. cayenne powder
- Food processor
- 1 tbsp. onion powder
- 2 tsp. Thyme

- 1/3 cup Red Bell pepper, diced

Dough

- 1/2 tsp. oregano
- 3/4 cup Spring Water
- 1/2 cup Garbanzo Bean Flour
- 1 tsp. Sea Salt
- 1/2 tsp. Basil

- 1 1/2 cup Spelt Flour

cheese

- Blender (Blending cup preferred)
- 1/2 cup Spring Water
- 1/2 tsp. oregano
- 1/2 tsp. cayenne
- 1/2 cup Soaked Brazil Nuts (Soaked for a few hours)
- 2 tsp. onion powder

- 1 tsp. Sea Salt

This recipe can be greatly enjoyed alongside alkaline tomato sauce.

Direction for preparation

1. Grab your food processor. Set aside your garbanzo bean flour then add all other filling ingredients to your food

processor. allow to blend for 30 seconds then mix it in flour till its thoroughly blended.

2. Set your cooker to medium heat, place a skillet on it then cast the skillet lightly with grapeseed oil.
3. Next, spread out your ravioli filling, allow each side to cook for 4 minutes.
4. Break up the filling, cook it again for some minutes before setting it aside in a bowl
5. Grab your blender, toss in cheese ingredients and allow to blend thoroughly until it is smooth. add spring water if it's too thick.
6. Grab your food processor, place all the dry dough ingredients in it then allow it to blend for 10 seconds. Drizzle water into the mix while blending until the dough forms a ball. alternatively, if you do not have a food processor, you can mix the ingredients in a bowl then knead until it forms a ball.
7. Sprinkle flour on your working area then roll ¼ dough in your palm. add flour as needed.
8. Get a bowl, mix filling and cheese in it. Thereafter, spoon the mixture on one side of the dough about ½ apart.
9. Fold the dough over and pat it down around filling, use pastry cutter to cut out ravioli, ensure that each ravioli is sealed.(The ravioli can be frozen for later use)
10. Boil spring water, add sea salt and some oil, then, cook ravioli for 6 minutes.
11. once the cooking is done, drain out the water then allow the ravioli to cool down before serving.
12. Serve with alkaline tomato sauce if you wish.

DR. SeBI BLUeBeRRY SpeLT paNcaKeS RecIpe

This recipe is just enough for 12 pancakes

Ingredients

- 1/2 cup Blueberries
- 1/4 tsp. Sea Moss or Dr. Sebi's plus Bromide powder (optional) *
- Grapeseed oil
- 1/2 cup Spring Water (optional)
- 2 tbsp. Grapeseed* (updated from 1/2 cup)
- 1/2 cup agave
- 2 cups Spelt Flour
- 2 tbsp. Hemp Seeds
- 1 cup Hemp Milk or approved Nut Milk

- *If you use sea moss as gel, the batter will be very sticky.*

Direction for preparation

1. Grab a large bowl then set aside your hemp milk. Mix grapeseed oil, agave, sea moss, hemp seeds and spelt flour in the bowl. (Do not add the hemp milk to what you are mixing as it may form lumps when it comes in contact with grapeseed oil).
2. To get the consistency you want, mix in 1 cup of hemp milk then add water as required.
3. The blueberries should be folded into a batter.
4. Set your cooker to medium heat then coat lightly with grapeseed oil.
5. pour out the batter into the skillet. allow them to cook for 5 minutes on each side.
6. Your blueberry spelt pancake is now ready to be served.

If you want your pancake to be more cooked, set your oven to 350 °F then bake for few minutes.

While making your pancakes, you can substitute any of the ingredients with other Dr. Sebi approved nut milks, fruits and flours.

DR. SeBI VeGaN oMeLeT RecIpe

This recipe will yield a maximum of 1 omelet.

Ingredients

- 1/4 cup chopped Mushrooms
- 1/4 cup diced Green pepper
- 1/4 tsp. Sea Salt
- 1/4 tsp. oregano
- 1/4 tsp. onion powder
- Brazil Nut cheese (optional)
- 1/4 tsp. Sweet Basil
- Grapeseed oil
- 1/4 tsp. cayenne powder
- 1/4 cup Garbanzo Bean Flour
- 1/4 cup diced Roma Tomato
- 1/3 cup Spring Water

- 1/4 cup chopped onion

To get this recipe right, you must be careful while flipping. If anything goes wrong while you are flipping, you can make it into alkaline veggie scramble. Depending on how much vegetables you prefer in your omelet. You might not have the need for all the chopped and diced vegetables.

Direction for preparation

1. Grab a medium sized bowl then whisk seasonings, water and flour in it.
2. Set your cooker to medium heat, place a skillet on it then add 1 tablespoon of grapeseed oil to the skillet.
3. Take a spoonful of each vegetable and tomatoes and saute in the skillet for 3 minutes.
4. pour out your egg mixture into the skillet, allow it to cook for 4 minutes before flipping.
5. While the egg is in the skillet, lift the sides of the omelet lightly then tilt towards the lifted area to allow the mixture get to the bottom of the skillet to cook.
6. Make use of your spatula to flip the omelet, afterwards, add Brazil nut cheese on half of the omelet then fold it over.

7. Your alkaline veggie omelet is now ready to be served.

DR. SeBI aVocaDo pIZZa SaUce RecIpe

Ingredients

Measurements:

- 1/2 tsp. Sea Salt
- 1/2 tsp. onion powder
- 1 avocado
- pinch of Basil
- 2 tbsp. choppedonion
- 1/2 tsp. oregano.

Direction for preparation:

1.Divide the avocado in half, remove the pit and scoop out the insides into your food processor.

2.Take the rest of your ingredients and put it into your food processor. allow it to blend for 3 minutes or until its thoroughly blended. If it's necessary, scrape the inside of your food processor.

DR. SeBI aQUaFaBa RecIpe

Materials needed to prepare this Recipe

- Spring Water
- 1 tsp. Sea Salt

- Bag of Garbanzo Beans (chickpeas)

The remnant liquid from cooking chickpeas is what is referred to as aquafaba and it is mostly used as an alternative to eggs in certain recipes.

Ingredients

- 2 tbsp. aquafaba = 1 egg white
- 3 tbsp. aquafaba = 1 egg

- aquafaba is also one of the main ingredients in alkaline Whipped cream.

Direction for preparation

1. Grab a large pot, pour in spring water and bring to a boil. add salt and chickpeas.
2. Remove the pot from your cooker, set aside, cover with a lid and allow to sit for 45 minutes.
3. Drain off the water and leave the chickpeas sitting in the pot.
4. Set your cooker to medium heat, put the pot back on the cooker, add 6 cups of spring water then allow to cook for 1 hour 30 minutes or until tender.
5. Drain off the water (aquafaba) and store in a glass jar. allow it to set in a refrigerator until its cool.

6. once the water in the jar has cooled down, there should be a certain thickness to it. If there is too much water in your aquafaba, boil for another 15 minutes.

Tomato pizza Sauce

Measurements:

- 1 tsp. oregano
- 5 Roma Tomatoes
- 1 tsp. onion powder
- pinch of Basil
- 2 tbsp. agave
- 2 tbsp of chopped onion
- 2 tbsp. Grape Seed oil

- 1 tsp. Sea Salt

Direction for preparation:

1.Make small x-shaped cuts on the ends of the plum tomatoes then place them in boiling water to a minute. This is to make it easy to remove the skin.

2.Dip the tomatoes in ice for 30 seconds. This will ease the removal of the skin.

3.Toss in the tomatoes into your blender then blend for 30 seconds or until a smooth texture is achieved.

DR. SeBI STRaWBeRRY BaNaNa Ice cReaM RecIpe

This recipe can only make a maximum of 1 quart of ice cream.

Ingredients

- 1 cup Frozen Strawberries
- 1 tbsp. agave
- 1/4 cup Nut/Hemp Milk
- Blender
- 5 Frozen Baby Bananas
- 1/2 of avocado

Frozen fruits is optional but it will allow the ice cream set faster if you use it.

avocado is recommended in the list of fruits to add as the fat from it makes the ice cream creamier. You can add other fruits of your choosing too.

Direction for preparation

1. Grab your blender, toss in all the ingredients then blend until well mixed.
2. Take a pinch out of the ingredients then taste for sweetness and texture. add more agave if it needs more sweetness or more milk if it is too thick.
3. Scoop into an air-tight container and freeze for 6 hours until its firm.
4. Your ice cream is ready to be scooped and served.

*If the ice cream is too hard to scoop out, allow it to soften for a few minutes. Then try to scoop again.